FALL

AS THE EARTH TURNS

Lynn M. Stone

The Rourke Book Co., Inc.
Vero Beach, Florida 32964

Edited by Sandra A. Robinson

PHOTO CREDITS
All photos © Lynn M. Stone

Library of Congress Cataloging-in-Publication Data

Stone, Lynn M.
  Fall / by Lynn M. Stone.
    p. cm. — (As the earth turns)
  Includes index.
  ISBN 1-55916-019-5
  1. Autumn—Juvenile literature. [1. Autumn.]
I. Title. II. Series: Stone, Lynn M. As the earth turns.
QB637.7.S76 1994
508—dc20   93-39057
                                                CIP
                                                AC

Printed in the USA

TABLE OF CONTENTS

FALL

The fall, or autumn, season follows summer and leads to winter. Our first fall calendar day is either September 22 or 23, depending upon the year. In many parts of North America, the signs of fall begin earlier than that.

Fall brings cooler weather and shorter periods of sunlight. It also brings changes in the ways that plants and animals live.

Fall colors brighten riverbanks on an early October morning in Vermont

THE SUN AND THE SEASONS

The Earth journeys in an **orbit** around the sun once each year. The Earth's motion causes its tilt, or angle, toward the sun to change slightly each day. As the angle changes, the amount of sunlight reaching Earth changes, and the weather and seasons change, too. This is why daylight lasts longer in July, for example, than it does in November.

Animals like this marmot in Washington have to hustle to fatten up and beat autumn's countdown to winter

FALL NORTH AND SOUTH

During our fall and winter, the northern **hemisphere,** or half, of the Earth is tilted away from the sun. At the same time, the southern hemisphere is tilting toward the sun. That means spring begins in the southern hemisphere when autumn begins in the northern.

The southern hemisphere's fall begins in March, when spring begins in the north.

Autumn browns once-green
mountain meadows and
calls bighorn rams to battle

FALL ARRIVES

Fall in the northern hemisphere arrives in early September. Days are warm, but shorter than in summer. Nights are cooler, and mornings are often wet with dew.

Soon the days are cool, too. One morning the ground is covered with frost instead of dew.

By November, skies are gray more often than blue. Winds shake leaves from branches and the first snowflakes swirl. Autumn is passing into winter.

An elk calf stands in a meadow painted by Jack Frost's brush

Fall arrives early in September on the tundra of Alaska

Indian corn, apples and pumpkins — an autumn harvest

THE LEAVES OF FALL

The growing seasons end in fall for most green plants. Plants dry and die — but before the land turns from green to brown, autumn "paints" a spectacular scene.

Chemical changes turn leaves from green to gold, fiery red, orange and purple. The scene lasts a few magical weeks in September and October. Then the leaves float down in autumn's wind and rain.

Fall's bold, bright leaves color a hillside in Vermont

ANIMALS IN FALL

Animals fatten up in early fall. In late autumn, animals such as bears and **marmots hibernate.** They enter a deep sleep until spring.

As autumn leaves fall, birds **migrate,** or travel, to distant, warmer places. There they will find food all winter. Meanwhile, bats fly to winter dens. Frogs and turtles burrow into the mud.

Wild geese leave northern cornfields in late autumn and migrate south

FALL FIGHTS

For wild male animals with horns or antlers, fall is a time to fight. The strongest males take the females as mates. Male deer, elk, moose and bighorn sheep decide which is strongest by fighting others of their kind.

Bull elks bugle challenges to each other in mountain meadows. Above the meadows, the cracking sound of bighorn rams butting heads echoes.

A bull elk bellows a challenge to his rivals

FALL MEANS ...

Fall means harvesting apples, pumpkins, grapes and **gourds.** It means the smoky haze of burning leaves and the glitter of a morning frost.

Fall means the roar of a crowd in a football stadium, the World Series, chilled cider and the sound of pheasant wings.

Fall means V-shaped flights of wild geese. Fall means flowers like chrysanthemums.

Fall means the hush of a lonely, country road

FALL AROUND THE WORLD

The brilliant show of fall leaves we enjoy in much of North America doesn't happen everywhere.

In places closer to the **equator,** all the seasons are much alike. The equator is an imaginary line around the Earth's middle. There the Earth's angle toward the sun changes very little.

Southern Florida is close enough to the equator to feel like summer all year long.

Glossary

equator (ee KWAY ter) — the imaginary line drawn on maps around the Earth's middle at an equal distance from the north and south poles

gourd (GORD) — any one of several squash and squashlike fruits

hemisphere (HEHM iss fear) — either the northern or southern half of the Earth, using the equator as a divider

hibernate (HI ber nate) — to enter a long, deep winter sleep during which the animal's normal body functions are slowed

marmot (MAR mutt) — a large ground squirrel of the mountains in western North America; the western form of the woodchuck or groundhog

migrate (MI grate) — to travel at the same time each year to the same distant place, usually to reach more plentiful food

orbit (OR bit) — the path that an object follows as it repeatedly travels around another object in space

INDEX